Just Beautiful

Also by Tim Suermondt

The Dangerous Women with Their Cellos (1998)

Greatest Hits 1988-2001 (2002)

Trying to Help the Elephant Man Dance (2007)

Just Beautiful

Tim Suermondt

Books™

The New York Quarterly Foundation, Inc.
New York, New York

NYQ Books™ is an imprint of The New York Quarterly Foundation, Inc.

The New York Quarterly Foundation, Inc.
P. O. Box 2015
Old Chelsea Station
New York, NY 10113

www.nyqbooks.org

Copyright © 2010 by Tim Suermondt

All rights reserved. No part of this book may be used or reproduced in any manner whatsoever without written permission of the author. This book is a work of fiction. Any references to historical events, real people or real locales are used fictitiously. Other names, characters, places, and incidents are products of the author's imagination, and any resemblance to actual events or locales or persons, living or dead, is entirely coincidental.

First Edition

Set in New Baskerville

Layout and Design by Raymond P. Hammond
Cover Photo ©2010 Constance Norgren
Cover Layout and Design by Jarriett K. Robinson

Library of Congress Control Number: 2010907953

ISBN: 978-1-935520-28-3

For Pui, again.

Acknowledgments

The New York Quarterly

Poetry East

Southern Humanities Review

Indiana Review

River Styx

Cider Press Review

5 AM

Atlanta Review

Off The Coast

River Oak Review

The Cortland Review

Painted Bride Quarterly

Green Hills Literary Lantern

Ship Of Fools

Clark Street Review

Rattle

Cold Mountain Review

3rd Wednesday

Contents

I

It's the Drifting   / 15
Graduation   / 16
Bon Voyage   / 17
"Fire in Houston Blamed on Inflatable Gorilla"   / 18
Why Art Always Trumps Commerce   / 20
Right Field   / 21
Looking Forward Boldly   / 22
Good Jokes   / 23
The Lingering Intention of the World   / 24
Taking Stock   / 25
The Sixties   / 26
The History of Folk Music   / 27
Thanksgiving   / 28
Ars Poetica   / 29
Wondering   / 30
The Dolphins   / 31
Humanity is Such a Large Subject   / 32
New Year's, 2010   / 33
Your Return   / 34
Trivial importance   / 35
What Would He Ever Do   / 36
Bright, Brighton Beach   / 37
Eddie's Chariot Just as Sweet   / 38
The Lyricism I Don't have   / 39
Red Hot   / 40
We Do at City Hall   / 41

II

It Had to Happen   /45
Just Beautiful   / 46
The Kind of Day   / 47
With the Birds on Ascan Avenue   / 48
The Magic Marko   / 49
President Suermondt   / 50
Einstein Looks in the Window   / 51
In Some Country, Anytime   / 52
Mr. Pinochet   / 53
Real Men   / 54
Don't You Worry   / 55
The Killing of the Birds   / 56
Delray   / 58
Pancho Villa Returns His Suit to Me   / 59
The Neighbor Reads Celan in Jo Ann's Beauty Parlor   / 60
The Master Builder   / 61
Neruda's House in a Dream   / 62
Simone Weil on the Ferris Wheel...   / 63
Still Punching   / 64
Van Gogh's Room in Auvers is Driving Him Crazy   / 66
Hollywood   / 67
Watching a Favorite Twilight Zone Episode...   / 68
Well, it's a History of Philosophy   / 69
The Big Pierre   / 70
The Preparation   / 71
The Lost Cause Revisited   / 72
Ten People at the Poetry Reading   / 73
Such Expectations   / 74

III

The Pursuit of Happiness / 77
A Pinch of Genius if You're Lucky / 78
Supreme / 79
A History of Baseball / 80
What does it Mean? / 81
Comforting the Doubts of Science and Moving On /82
A City Boy's Pastoral / 83
Winning the Pulitzer / 84
Poems: Old and Random / 85
Valentine's Day / 86
Baluga Street / 87
City for the Taking / 88
Fallujah / 89
The Butterflies of Walking / 90
Hearing Aid for the Younger / 92
Every City That's Ever been / 93
Pasta / 94
Absolutely / 95
A Man and the Serious World / 96
The Sound of Money Leaving / 97
Counting on One / 98
Even in Paris / 99
Splendid for the New Life / 100
Dancers Going Far / 101
On the Street Leading to the Mean Streets / 102
After the Election / 103
Hong Kong Hui / 104
The Present and the Future / 105

*Today I just want to tell you
that the bedside lamp from your room
was promoted to star.*

—Ewa Lipska

I

IT'S THE DRIFTING

When I read the laments
over authors who are no longer in print,
I wish I were able to arouse more sympathy.
In my case it's usually about
trying to get into print in the first place.
It's somewhat like rafting in that it's not
the raft, but the drifting that's important—
the slow as sloth movements, sure, but
also the sheer moments of speeding light,
that bullet train in our minds, the worlds
we think we might love going by,
the days full of colors we've never seen,
the nights of falling stars turning the rivers
white as snow and bone, the accumulation
of everything real and unreal that prompted
us to write it down from the very beginning.

GRADUATION

All the things the young will do and see
that I never will.
All the things I've seen and done
that they never will—the trade-off
seems fair.
I walk down the block,
the elms lined up
like they are on inspection—
"Those shoes need more shine,
Suermondt," the sun hanging
over my shoulder as if it cares.

BON VOYAGE

The man gets out of bed,
goes into the backyard and attempts
to fly like the kid dashing
from the movies, eager to soar
like the people on the screen.
Where the boy failed, the man succeeds—
his body, long and serious
like a Spanish saint in an El Greco,
shuttles above the neighborhood
peaceful at this hour as the cemetery.
He comes down in a part of the city
he's heard of, but never been to—
a group of toughs who see him land
break out in applause and call him boss.
The man makes his way home, puts on
a kettle of coffee and summons the courage
to tell his wife what happened—
if it doesn't win her back, at least
give her pause, it *will* be over.
The flying by comparison was easy. Amazing.

"FIRE IN HOUSTON BLAMED ON INFLATABLE GORILLA"

It's all he wanted—
to buy a pair of jeans
and some cowboy boots.
He didn't realize that a blowup
gorilla can scare people
as much as a real gorilla.

So he made his way
to the roof of a store
at the Mall, hoping he might
come up with an answer
as to why those
who are a little odd—
or very odd—are subjected
to the worst misunderstandings.

As he contemplated,
a piece of debris punctured
a hole in him—he deflated
quickly, strips of rubber
clinging to the tops
of the security lights,
setting the roof ablaze—
the Fire Chief said
"He never had a chance."

Think of all the times
your heart has been punctured
and deflated, strewn
in a hundred pieces—

burnt to a crisp over a simple
wish you're embarrassed
to have to admit you didn't get.

A pair of jeans
and some cowboy boots—
was it so much to ask for?

WHY ART ALWAYS TRUMPS COMMERCE

The young woman who plays her cello
by the park during lunchtime
has me transported and I forget the pain
at losing the Rochester account—

I'm feeling what Pablo Casals must have felt
when he was allowed to return to Spain.
I'm marching with Bei Dao into the new city
and I'm there with Tobias

when he finds his long lost son.
I want to drop to my knees and kiss the ground—
such happiness in being alive.
I put bills in the woman's tips box

and glance up at the tall buildings,
buildings I could easily jump or fly over,
buildings I no longer find callous and sterile—
I'm taking the stairs to my fifth floor office.

RIGHT FIELD

I'm out of place
but at home.

I hear "has-been"
whistling in the wind

and convinced I see
a vulture circling above.

But I have no inclination
to fuss over worry.

I pound my glove
and stand erect as a prince,

royal in my nonchalance,
although there's a tiny

bend at the knees.
If I do stumble

on the first pitch hit at me,
I can say I lost

it in the clouds
like Willie Mays once said,

still young enough to make
excuses means being still

young enough. Batter up—
it's been a long time.

LOOKING FORWARD BOLDLY

> *Almost all my friends*
> *have become blackbirds.*
> —Eugen Jebeleanu

A few will become hawks and eagles—
the one who owes me money will become

a buzzard if he doesn't pay—standard
punishment. I expect my wife and I will

become kingfishers, diving in the deep waters,
wet and hungry every day, pecking ourselves

clean on the most beautiful of beaches.

GOOD JOKES

My father didn't have a good sense of humor
which is why I brought along good jokes
whenever I paid him a visit.
He always endured them with forbearance
and at the end always, always said: "That one
wasn't bad at all." Since he believed that justice
will triumph (as I do too), I'm sure he's enjoying
the afterlife and the people there who tell him jokes.
Maybe one night after dinner
in his heavenly bungalow, he'll gather my mother
and uncle and some angels who've been designated
to oversee the racetracks and stock markets—
gather them in the living room and announce
he's going to tell a joke, a joke of mine.
My mother and uncle will beam, the angels will
take notes—my father will clear his throat and begin:
"A man walks into a shoe store..." Oh that one
wasn't bad, wasn't bad at all.

THE LINGERING INTENTION OF THE WORLD

It enjoys annoying us
in the simplest ways,
without breaking a sweat—
evidence in the leaves
you keep raking, and raking.
Even your love's teasing
("You missed some yellow
ones over there")
can't save the day.
You curse Keats for worshipping
autumn, for dying young
before he could become
wise enough to take it back.

TAKING STOCK

I'm at the point in my life
where I don't have to worry
about the point in my life.

Whatever happens, I can
view the results dispassionately—
well almost. I am getting there.

Hot Triumph and Cold Defeat
are holding hands on the couch.
What a cute couple.

Let them sort it out
and give me the destination.
I'm writing on a yellow pad—

words of possible worth
or nothing, in any event.

THE SIXTIES

Much smoke and mirrors,
burning bras of the decade

    yet

leavened with sparks
of the extraordinary,

moving like Pete Maravich—
"I can't believe I saw

    what I just didn't see."

THE HISTORY OF FOLK MUSIC

Woody Guthrie knocks on my door:
"Tim, can I have my guitar back?
Can I have it back, please?"
I wish I had his guitar to give back,
I really do, but you can't go anywhere
anymore on a freight train anyway.

THANKSGIVING

The world outside is as brutal and beautiful as ever.
Sunday is Sunday and again in the middle of the day
My wife and I are lying together on the couch.
A pro football game is on the TV and the sound is off.
The books on the coffee table are simple and to the point.
My wife stirs lightly in her robe and wraps her arms around me.
She says she's happy with the door painted blue.

ARS POETICA

I'm helping the contractor
cut strips of carpeting
and stapling them
onto the stair's steps.
He tells me he wrote
long poems in high school,
doing his best to make
them indecipherable—
"I figured if anyone
understood the poems,
they weren't poems at all."
"There's a lot of that
going around today," I say,
"and poets win prizes for it."
I'm curious what he'd say
about my poems, then decide
I'll settle for a stiff drink
when the work is done.
"Wasn't it Eliot," he asks,
"who said poetry doesn't
make a damn thing happen?"
"That was Auden." "Yeah,
yeah. Do you see any more
staples lying around?"

WONDERING

Tonight I'm wondering about the Southern Cross
and what Camus would have written
had he lived long enough to grow old
and how I wish I was the one to have written:
"She wore chaste dresses and yet her body burned."

I'm also wondering why Don Juan couldn't remember
the name of a single one of his many lovers
and why we can't let go of the belief that our politicians
have our best interests at heart and is the Vice- Presidency
truly worth only "a warm bucket of spit."

Frankly, I wonder a lot. My wife has gotten quite adept
at explaining to people that I'm not ignoring them,
"Tim's merely wondering" and if one of them should ask
"Wondering about what?" she'll say in the sweetest tone
with the sweetest expression imaginable: "I wonder."

THE DOLPHINS

> *Football isn't life and death.*
> *It's more important than that.*
> —Vince Lombardi

My brothers and I have taken over the living room,
cheering on Marino, Clayton, Duper and the rest
of the Miami Dolphins, hoping their porous defense
can hold the San Diego Chargers to under 30 points.
    My youngest brother's wife insists on preparing
the feast and my brothers and I take care of the cold beer
and horseplay. Just yesterday we were asking if our lives
were going somewhere or nowhere, but that sobering
concern has been batted down at the line of scrimmage
        and unceremoniously carted off the field.
Look at Mark Clayton out jumping the safety for the ball
and falling into the end zone. Falling into the end zone...
that's what it's all about, brothers, even after many years,
even if we make it in with far less flair and majesty.

HUMANITY IS SUCH A LARGE SUBJECT

You could be given
a million lives
and remain on the outskirts.
Something I like to remember
when I jump in
with my two left feet,
when love's manifold manifestations
beat my ass
and leave it under a lonely bridge.
It works for me.

NEW YEAR'S, 2010

Another year older—it's just what I needed.
Not that I'm complaining—alright, I'm complaining.
But hope still abounds. My wife and I will pop
A bottle of champagne, drink to the health
Of the newlyweds we are and slow dance
In the living room. She sees the blond in my hair—
And insists she doesn't require a microscope.

YOUR RETURN

Rosebuds cling to the windows
to get the best view.

    Creatures move toward the house gingerly
    as if the ground were eggshells
    and they have to make sure they don't fall through
    before you arrive.

I put on a clean shirt,
wait by the door.
Put my hands in my pockets
and try to come up with a few lyrical words

    to spring on you
    as soon as the door opens…

The sun seems anxious too,
shining in anticipation like you wouldn't believe.

TRIVIAL IMPORTANCE

If he's not the King of Trivia
he's next in line. It's astounding
the way he brings the minutiae forth
without a moment's hesitation.
A professor on a national cable show
claimed this is exactly the skill
that keeps us stupid and, I suppose,
enabled the head of the Noble Prize
to single out American writers
as irrelevant to the wider world.
One would think—he would think—
that any intelligent man or woman
attuned to tragedy's high ability
to waylay us all would be more
understanding and wise: Dobie Gillis
never hurt a soul and his dad didn't
mean it when he said: "I'm going to
kill that boy." May we be so lucky.

WHAT WOULD HE EVER DO

In the second floor bedroom
my wife sits by the window,
writing in her notebook.
The dark weather
starts to brighten
and the blue jays appear again.
On the ground floor
I play the music that prompted
her to climb the stairs
and find her corner getaway.
I fumble-step through the kitchen
like a dancer missing his partner.
"What would he ever do
without me?" she writes with flourish,
with her exquisite timing.

BRIGHT, BRIGHTON BEACH

The grandmothers and grandfathers
wear their thick Khrushchev and Brezhnev
overcoats even on a Summer's day.

The girls wear jeans from the Gap
and the boys model their sandy hair
after the latest Hollywood and Moscow

film heartthrob. "Russia Along the Sea"
along the boardwalk, serves hamburgers,
borscht and pigs in a blanket.

American flags hang with the flags
of the Russian Republic and the sad, black
flags remembering the Prisoners of War.

At the PY3AHHA grocery store, a cartoon
Stalin shares window space with a New York
Mets logo: "This Is The Year We Win It All"

EDDIE'S CHARIOT JUST AS SWEET

My father puts on his sneakers
And takes his favorite walk

For the last time. The day
Welcomes him with honey-colored

Sky. People call and wave
And my father calls and waves

Back—"a kingly act," he once
Remarked, "a castle of friendship."

My father strolls along the river,
A slower but steady oar.

He looks out over the water
Until he feels death gliding

Toward him like a swan. He sits
On a bench—what wind there is

Ruffles his hair like a lover's
Hand. My father closes his eyes

And in a doorway my mother
Stands with the patience of eternity:

"Come in, sweetheart. I can't keep
Your meatloaf warm forever."

THE LYRICISM I DON'T HAVE

I'm with Milosz on this one:
I can't be blamed—I've done
what I could, but anyone checking
the definition of "meat and potatoes"
will see my picture along side,
my sly grin doing all it can
to hide my obvious deficiency.
If I lived in Suzhou, where legend
claims the most beautiful women
in China live—they would ignore me,
secure in their knowledge
that I'm an escapee from the iron works,
completely unfit to be graceful.
I'd continue to write love poems
to them all, poems more rawhide
than silk, more harsh yellow sun
than glorious yellow moon.
I'd travel the water-towns, the alleyways,
alone in simple dress, my rough
arms swinging like clumsy songbirds.

RED HOT

Love comes in handy in a blighted world
And there's plenty here at the Chinese restaurant
Where my wife and I are celebrating
The anniversary of our first dinner date.

The light from the Vietnamese sandwich shop
Across the street beams on the snow and slush
That has been shoveled to the curb.

A man walking by our window balances a small
Pizza box with one hand, holding a boy's
Hand with the other while Prince Chi-Liu rides
Down the street in a golden Second Dynasty boat—

He's searching for love and deliverance.
Come back, what you're looking for is here
Swirling around my general tso chicken
And my wife's soft, perfect dumplings.

WE DO AT CITY HALL

I put a ring on your finger,
you put a ring on mine

but the lame remained lame.
The blind still couldn't see.
Peace didn't break out—

Elvis stayed dead.

"How can the world be so stupid?"
we said to each other.

II

IT HAD TO HAPPEN

> *I accepted the inevitable: I became an adult.*
> —Octavio Paz

I locked up my comic books
and my Little League bat.

I worked on my vocabulary
and became quite adroit

at using the word "ubiquitous"
in many of my conversations.

I wore a cut-rate fancy suit
and played the Market well.

I took a blonde scientist dancing
and she taught me the Cosmos.

I quit while I was far ahead
and went boating off Cape Cod.

I championed every exile
and learned to love my white hair.

I once bumped my wife in the night
and told her about the Masked Marvel.

JUST BEAUTIFUL

A popular and beautiful actress
comes out of the chic clothing store—
into the sun.

She wants to be the sun.

I'm so close I could touch her
and though later I'll dismiss

the overheated business of beauty
and every notion of fame

I'm enthralled watching her, bound
by a tight blouse and tight skirt,
wiggle to a waiting limo.

For an instant, I catch my reflection
blithe and orange in the tinted window
and a convincing voice in my head

says: "You could have been big
in Pictures. Look at this close-up,
just fine, just beautiful."

I love my anonymous life.

THE KIND OF DAY

for Rachel Wetzsteon

The man and woman are sitting
on a bench along the Hudson,
each eating a deli bought
ham sandwich and sharing
a bottle of seltzer water.

She tells him she's happy
he found someone
and he tells her she will
too—he believes time
will prove generous to both of them,
and why not on such a day—

the kind of day that makes
the sludge around the pilings
look like dark chocolate,
the kind of day that makes
sad New Jersey in the distance
look almost beautiful.

WITH THE BIRDS ON ASCAN AVENUE

On my way to the funeral home
I'm accosted by hundreds of birds.

I start thinking Hitchcock
only to switch to Francis of Assisi

as it becomes clear that the birds
mean me no harm.

They provide escort for the last
two blocks, flying away

when I reach the door. I ring
the bell, ready to receive my father's

ashes. My father who I suspect
has left here days ago,

having fashioned his own wings
capable of soaring higher

than birds can imagine.
While I sit in the main office

I notice two cardinals balleting
onto a branch, bowing their heads

as if in choreographed
tribute. I'd like to tell you I see

my father flying by but, even in a poem,
you can't, can't have everything.

THE MAGIC MARKO

At twelve I pulled—
not rabbits—but ducks
out of a top hat.

My pals asked
how I did it
and I wouldn't tell.

Now, I don't remember
the secret and haven't
given any thought

to finding it and attempting
a re-creation, fearing
that whatever animal

or thing I pull
out of the hat would be puny,
at best, and disappoint

The Magic Marko who's very
much alive in memory.
The top hat is in one

of the boxes in a room
on the tiny second floor.
It probably thinks it's useless,

a sentiment I understand, but
a vestige of magic is magic—
abracadabra, yes.

PRESIDENT SUERMONDT

Every Sunday a different group
of crippled soldiers visits me
in the Oval office,

soldiers who've been braver
in one minute than I have been
in my life so far.

Usually one soldier will wind up
saying: "President Suermondt.
It has a great ring to it"—

and it does, sorry modesty.
Every Sunday I take the soldiers
out to the Rose Garden

where their bodies are again made
whole, the clicking in of limbs
a sound impossible to surpass.

The soldiers take the wonder
in stride, as if the wars
meant for this to happen too.

Usually one of them, rising from
a wheelchair, will wind up
saying: "Thank you, Mr. President"

and shake my hand, and we'll
all stroll the grounds, smartly,
until the evening finally comes.

EINSTEIN LOOKS IN THE WINDOW

It's easy conjuring him up, easy
as conjuring up beer and pizza—
and the woman in the summer dress
who's waving all the time from everywhere.

In a world of uncertainty Einstein was certain:
"God doesn't gamble with the Universe,"
he said—a statement I take seriously
since the last horse I bet on

is still running as I write this—
I hope she makes it to the finish line
before the first snow comes.
I go to the window just in case

Einstein is there—a bird the vivid color
of pepperoni lands on the sill, pecks
feverishly on the glass then flies off
which I take as a sign I should get outside

where perhaps the woman in the summer dress
will join me, even say: "Tim, you're a genius,
like Einstein"—while the entire neighborhood,
my dazzling planet, fans to spread the news.

IN SOME COUNTRY, ANYTIME

Wearing a neat disguise
the Dictator visits the bookshop
on the outskirts of the capital city.
He wonders why he came, aware
there's precious worth reading—
his orders have seen to that.
He wonders why he allows
the bookshop to exist at all.
Yet when he sees his
autobiography, ghostwritten
years ago, he's forced to admit
a sense of pride. He browses
a bit, like a tourist trying
to prove he's not as out of place
as he is. He notices a book titled
Machines for the Glory of the State
and sighs, and leaves
without responding to the owner's
"Please come back again soon."
He decides to walk along the canal
which was once very lovely
but is now rather polluted, still
showing traces of blood.
He rests on a scarred bench
and pulls a sandwich from his jacket
pocket, slowly unwrapping the wax
paper. "I know I'm a small man,"
he says, flattering himself. "We all are."

MR. PINOCHET

Everyone tells me I was a dictator
but I'm sure I wasn't. No, no.
For all the months
I've been sunning myself
in my wheelchair on the balcony
of my hospital room, butterflies
have come to me, and I've pulled
wings off of only 2, maybe 3, or 4, or 5.
I think, No, no, I know
I am a barber—I own
a small shop in Estavos—
I can touch the yellow awning
and I'm certain I charge a fair price
for a clip and a close shave.
Of course, my therapist says
a tango teacher is a distant possibility.
Yes, yes. I work well with people
and oh how I loved to dance.

REAL MEN

They try to be kinder
but find the transition impossible—
"I can't figure out
this here mechanism."

They come home from the factories,
the offices and the fields
and wonder how some folks
believe the Universe makes sense.

They tell the children that candy
costs money and must be earned
before a few pieces are passed out.

They sit at the dinner table—
say little or stay silent as stone,
trying to appear as strong as oxen
and their wives white porcelain plates.

DON'T YOU WORRY

Mary and Joseph fussed over the babe
like any other parents absorbed in the ritual excess:
light tickling, oohs and ahs, the insufferable baby talk.
To get their attention, the Guardian Angel had to tap them
hard on the shoulder, pull them to the side.
"Listen, when you start noticing your son doing things
you don't understand, don't you worry. Learning to become
the King of the Jews is not always going to be
a picnic at the bazaar."
"I'm not worried," Joseph said.
"I'm not worried," said Mary.
"Thank God," said the Angel, "makes my job much easier."
As he stepped around them and flapped his wings, the Angel
discharged one more piece of advice, "Don't ever forget this:
There isn't anything fair about life," and lifted off
right through the stable roof.
"Now I'm worried," Mary said.
"Don't worry," said Joseph, "if our Jesus turns out to be
a lousy carpenter, he'll need something to fall back on."

THE KILLING OF THE BIRDS

A scholar Pope orders
the birds in the Vatican garden
killed because they disturb
his contemplations.

I mention this
not to disparage the Popes—
some were better, some were worse
and somehow gratitude

always trumps bitterness
if you assert it does. So let's remember
the Birdman of Flatbush
(superior to the one of Alcatraz)

teaching his parrot sweet defiance
by getting it to jabber:
"Polly doesn't want a cracker."
Hitchcock would have given assent.

There's also Audubon, Francis of Assisi
and Judy the cancer girl
coolly coaxing an array of birds
to come visit her ward room—

a true story once well known.
Say this for the birds:
unlike angels, they make
the prospect of having wings and flying

seem more practical, immediate,
to some minds certainly,
an addition to the earth's ravishments
worth its weight in imagination.

A bird in the hand means worshipping both—
how this squares with the spiritual
I'll leave to the Pope
and that sparrow pecking his holy head.

DELRAY

for Greg Pape

The packinghouse's dim blue lights.
Fruit that keeps coming, and coming
On the conveyor belt, oranges and grapefruit
Jerking around on the wooden rollers
As if they have been electrocuted.

The women who remove the ones
With the slightest imperfections,
Their hands working in skillful consort,
Like surgeons they could have been
In another life, living rich and respected
In mansions on the beach.

The men who keep a lookout for the foreman
And watch the women at work, men known
By their monikers the women love...Professor
Slim, el Chu-chu, Felipe the Red and sad-eyed
Willie, the eternal Prince of Tin Cans.

PANCHO VILLA RETURNS HIS SUIT TO ME

"It is too big," he says
in his tough Mexican accent.
I tell him he's made a mistake
I can't help him
and I hope he won't be offended
as I ask him

why he, of all people,
would want to wear a suit.
"For my funeral," he says proudly.
"Pancho," I say, putting a hand
on his shoulder, "don't you know

you already died, a long time ago?"
"Si," he says, "when I died then
I had no suit.
Do you understand?"
I give him the name and address

of a tailor in town.
"A nip here, a tuck there
from Applebaum and your suit
will cling to you like a glove,
or a royal bandana."

He thanks me with a "Viva"
and veers off
like destiny itself often does:
dejected, feeling naked and alone,
searching for a change of history,
a suit, a suit that fits.

THE NEIGHBOR READS CELAN IN JO ANN'S BEAUTY PARLOR

She says she started reading Celan
for his humor
which of course is a joke—
yes, a little flippant

but it's one of the main
ingredients that justifies
comedy calling itself necessary.
While the beautician combs the hair

into the desired style, my neighbor
reads on with ease and purpose—
she's heartened that Celan travels well
anywhere, nobly here among the mists

of shampoos, perfumes
and the glossiest nail polish.
When the beautician finishes
and tells her "You look beautiful"

my neighbor, feeling like she's
journeyed quite a ways today,
closes the book gently
and doesn't have to say a word. She knows.

THE MASTER BUILDER

No one stacked the wooden boxes better.
He did it so well
you could use the word sharp
and not be off base.
At times he was so damn happy
with his building
he'd do a buck and a wing
Fred Astaire would have applauded.
This led to the nights
he'd tell himself
his ordinary supper
was fit for a king,
when he'd react to any mention
of "the downtrodden" on TV
by raising his hand: "Here, here,
don't leave me out!"—
nights when he'd dream
of a large house,
each brilliant room
filled with the loveliest women
begging him in for free.

NERUDA'S HOUSE IN A DREAM

The walls inside are blue,
blue as the sea just outside
and the berry bushes shad glow red

fudge their tips above the windowsills.
A poem is there on the table: another ode
to a naked woman, but it's signed—

what an uncanny stroke—with my name.
As I pick up the poem my body on the bed
turns quick, bumping the naked woman

luminous beside me. I know she's not there,
but she could be—she will be one day.
This could be a definition of poetry:

I'll accept it. I stare at the ceiling
and my vision pushes out among the stars
endless, irrepressible—I wonder if melancholy

and joy will still be locked in an embrace.
I wonder what houses, blue maybe bluer
than Neruda's will be found there.

SIMONE WEIL ON THE FERRIS WHEEL AT PLAZA DE LA CONCORDE

It's a consolation, after all.

STILL PUNCHING

When he was a young man
Harvey spent hours

punching the bag,
cocksure he'd develop

the talent to become
a welterweight champion.

It wasn't for lack of effort
that he failed. I'm a lover,

not a fighter—I can't say
if he gave up too early

as he feared he had.
At a party, Harvey went

out on the balcony
and began jabbing at the stars,

bap-bap-bap-bap,
light haloed around his fists.

We stopped and watched,
admiring the passion

and precision, and a woman
called out: "That's the kind

of fighting I like"—I liked
the elegant blows as well

and threw a couple of jabs
myself, awkward no doubt

in the execution, yet crisp
and lovely in the intent.

VAN GOGH'S ROOM IN AUVERS IS DRIVING HIM CRAZY

Keeps getting smaller and smaller—
feels at night like a jail cell.

He wants to run into the wheat fields
but realizes there's danger there too.

Doesn't want to be alone
yet only has toleration for Theo.

Wishes he had Gauguin's business acumen.
Wants to do a painting that sells.

Doesn't want to be forgotten
by the woman in yellow stockings.

Wants to believe he hears crows talking.
Doesn't want candles on his hat anymore.

Promises he'll throw away the pistol
wrapped in a drawer, soon.

HOLLYWOOD

for Charles Harper Webb

Talking heads, actors (some ex)
and directors
gabbing about movies
and the movies of...

This never happens
to poetry: "HOT POPSICLES
set the standard
in those days"—"Mark Strand's
first poem excited millions."

It's not our fault.

Poetry loves the underdog,
the hero who fails
and does so spectacularly—

our Hollywood, pal: Lonely,
often befuddled yet often brave
like Superman. Superman, old.

WATCHING A FAVORITE TWILIGHT ZONE EPISODE WITH PETE FAIRCHILD

We talk about the cheap special effects—
"Is Lloyd Bochner still alive?"—
we note that the female lab assistants
were always "bombshell babies," and how

could we have been taken in by To Serve Man.
Pete and I have common sense,
put to a vigorous practical use—
we know the inner workings of many things

(the mystery behind the mystery)—
we can hookup a jig on an Erco machine
quicker than the speed of light
and we're old enough to realize (now)

we should never have trusted an alien
who was Lurch in poor disguise—
yet when our imagination does rocket off
into outer space, it's okay. It'll reenter

back home to us in Binghamton or Los Angeles,
be as useful as an extra hammer or drill—
"We can have our spaceship and eat it too,"
Pete says. I agree, wishing I had said it first.

WELL, IT'S A HISTORY OF PHILOSOPHY

On the fading green court the tattooed young men
are playing basketball, badly again.
I have the damning misfortune to be living

in the neighborhood that spawns the worst
ballers. I'm half way between setting the book
aside and grabbing for my sneakers, but

decide I'll show them how it's done another day.
I read where Kant says something like "the idea
of God has to be an idea tough as an ax handle"—

like a power forward cleaning the glass, elbowing
the weaker into submission and the second row.
I dig this Immanuel, so much so I shout out

"You've got to get some philosophy, you've got
to move smooth" which the bumblers and bricklayers
below ignore, and I turn the page to the 19th Century.

THE BIG PIERRE

> *His umbrella was substantial.*
> —Henry Clay Wilkins
> on his law partner, Abraham Lincoln

Young and foolish,
I thought I had lost everything.

I swore the first poem
I sat down to write
would be my last—
but I outlived my youth.

I found out I did have
a few better angels
that were hard as nails
and completely devoted to me.

I bought a substantial umbrella
near the Hotel de Ville,
an umbrella wide enough
to protect all the people

of Paris and New York, an umbrella
I dubbed: The Big Pierre.

And since it's there at the ready
I don't worry about rain showers,
rainstorms—I don't even worry
about the future or oblivion.

Poems and poems yet to be
sit cluttered and hopeful
on my desk, waiting for overcast
skies—and a slight shaft of sun

to dance on the skylight.

THE PREPARATION

My mother was crawling peacefully
on the ceiling of her hospital room.

Before I could ask what was going on
she said "I'm trying to get a bit closer
to Heaven, sweetie, and getting used
to being up in the air."

It made perfect sense to me.

She was happy to hear I'd smuggled in
a bag of candies for her and told me
to have a seat: "I'll be down in a minute."

I sat on her bed, and wanting to do
something with my hands I reached
into the bag, pulled out a candy
and plopped it in my mouth.

It tasted so good I grabbed another one
and said "Take your time, Mom"
and she said she would.

THE LOST CAUSE REVISITED

Moonlight and Magnolia
and a basketball hoop
nailed to the Cypress tree.
Perfect.

TEN PEOPLE AT THE POETRY READING

No problem. Hide behind
the papers and the books
and imagine there are one hundred,
a thousand—let's make it
ten thousand. Ten thousand people
hanging on your every word
like a condemned convict waiting
on the last minute call from the Governor.
Ten thousand ready to carry you
to Parnassus, straight to
the palace formerly occupied
by Dante for centuries
before he moved into his new digs
roughly three months ago.
Pay scant attention at the reading's end
to the bald realization
that the roar of ten thousand
sounds like one hand clapping.
No problem. The Muse still loves you.

SUCH EXPECTATIONS

I step out the front door
    and there they are:

    my playmates from childhood,

standing and staring at me
    like the children in *The Village of the Damned,*

    the landscape suddenly desolate

as a starving dog. I say: "You haven't grown up"
    and blonde haired Sally Meissner

    says: "But you have" and wipes her nose

with the back of her hand. I backpedal inside,
    close the door and remain still for a few seconds,

    then take a peek out the living room window:

They're gone, not a trace. Orphans in the wind,
    I guess. Jesus, don't they know

    they have to grow up?

III

THE PURSUIT OF HAPPINESS

> *It is one step from the sublime*
> *to the ridiculous.*
> —Napoleon

I read a book on the Gulag
and thought myself a bit foolish
for thinking the world had ended
when my TV went out last month.

I remembered a frigid Wyoming winter
and could at least get a measured sense
of the weather conditions the prisoners
of the Kolyma were forced to try to endure.

I remembered the Osip Mandelstam line:
"the whole whore Moscow" and the business
about goldfinches hovering over the roof
like lost but still curious angels.

I convinced myself that the pursuit of happiness
was worthy of our serious attention and that
despair, damn shadow, is not supreme.
A candle or a TV. I've made my choice.

A PINCH OF GENIUS IF YOU'RE LUCKY

The way Mozart never
ran out of music and jokes.

The way Bobby Metcalf gobbled
up grounders at short...

the way they both died young.

The way failure finds the courage
to fail again and again.

The way my heart flies out
of my mouth like a red balloon

every time I stand in awe
of the most common occurrence.

SUPREME

> *It is only the unremarkable that will last.*
> —Larry Levis

The man who's talked off the ledge of the high-rise,
talked into giving life another try.

The gaunt woman who won't be mistaken for Beverly Sills,
singing opera daily in front of the bus yard.

Richard Nixon who gives his Checkers speech on the History Channel.

A HISTORY OF BASEBALL

When I took you home
you told me you'd "like to be married."
But between the living room
and the bedroom you decided
you were really moving in another direction.
For you it was a strategic reassessment.
For me it was as if a country
charmed with women in their white underwear
constantly on the lookout for me
had been destroyed forever.

When the following day I stepped
into the bright sunshine
I said "I will be able to cope"
with missing you in the world.
I felt like a career .209 hitter,
one who well after everyone is asleep
assumes a batting stance and never,
ever, fails to drive the ball
along the curvature of his imagination,
far into the night of outer space.

WHAT DOES IT MEAN?

On a fine June morning
I head out with my fishing rods,
the way a man should greet Summer.
My neighbor sprints up to me,
says his father will make it—
"Tim, he's such a hard-ass,
probably scared the damn Reaper to death."
Thinking of my father, I tell him
it makes sense, and I invite my neighbor
to come along down to the river
although he's begged off before—
"I'm no good fisherman."
This time he says okay
and all morning long
the fish flat-out leap at the bait.
"Wow, we can feed the whole town,"
my neighbor says, "What does it mean?"
Like astonishment itself I don't say
a word, just keep reeling them in.

COMFORTING THE DOUBTS OF SCIENCE AND MOVING ON

Wait, wait, listen to Physics,
don't force it, go slow—
be like Newton in his ease,
under the apple's glow.

A CITY BOY'S PASTORAL

In my Arcadia
a pizzeria stands prominently,
regally golden despite
some dishevelment.

Wisdom achieved every time
the cheese touches the tongue—

Contemplation rife in a field
of pepperoni with nary
a pesky dragonfly in sight.

A basketball hoop
instead of Pan's flute—

women in the shortest dresses
instead of leaf-clad nymphs.

Awe rising from the street
to the stars, flying into
the kitchen of the gods
or the lone Caesar:

"We who are about to eat
these slices, salute you!"

WINNING THE PULITZER

Don't laugh.
I have the chops.
I have the poems.
If I can outlast
the academic mumbo jumbo
I'll have a legitimate shot,
a puncher's chance.

At the awards ceremony
I'll thank everyone
who helped me, give the Bronx cheer
to everyone who never did

and return to my study
to write the next poem
like I always have and wanted to
oh those many years in the wilderness.

POEMS: OLD AND RANDOM

It's what I want my Collected poems to be called—
old as a lost painting in Venice
everyone is searching for—
random as a model's blush at 3 a.m. on Spring Street.

VALENTINE'S DAY

I'll make my dinner alone
and add a different, loving touch
for the occasion.

I'll sprinkle on basil,
toss in a few mushrooms
and change my brand of ketchup

to show I'm serious.
After the cutting and peeling,
the stirring and the frying,

I'll augment my meal
with a glass of red wine
cheap and tart.

I'll set a plate for Aphrodite
or the young woman
who inches up her skirt

whenever she passes by.
If one or both should
drop in on me,

I'll be on my best behavior.
I won't mention my fantasies.
I'll share the ketchup.

BALUGA STREET

On the corner a woman is running
her hands through her hair.

I was once with a woman
who loved running her hands
through her hair, and although
it must have been more
complicated, I think it's the reason
I fell in love with her
and believed it was meant to last.

I tell the woman on the corner
"I'm sorry. I know it wouldn't
have worked out between us,
but I love the way you run
your hands through your hair."

She utters "sweet of you"
and I resume walking. I've
forgotten where I wanted to go,
but I don't care. I look back
and the woman is still running
her hands through her hair—

we miss each other already.

CITY FOR THE TAKING

From the rooftop restaurant
the woman surveys the great city,
smaller but greater now
given her point of view:
"I was always a little afraid
of the city when I was a child," she says,
"but look, I can reach out
and pick up these tall buildings
like they were toys."
The man who's been preoccupied
with his Mexican chili sauce
says, "All you know about life
is what you know about life."
It's a joke, yet an explanation.
The woman brings a hand
lightly to her throat and laughs—
a red ribbon scuds through
the air, effortlessly.

FALLUJAH

"Keep me quiet like the stars"
you say, and instantly my mouth
seals itself over yours.
The world outside is bereft
and at war—I'm sorry, but what can one do?
You moan—I put my hand
under your panties and hear your heart
beating softly as a whisper
and I'm already wondering at the mystery
of what you'll cook for us come morning
when the neighbor's dog barks
again for its master, when the fish
belly sky shows its beautiful side.
This is all that matters tonight.

THE BUTTERFLIES OF WALKING

The poster actually read:
"The Benefits Of Walking."

I felt rather dumb
and tried to find
some consolation
by telling myself
it was just my eyes
getting a little bit older.

Yet I knew
this was a look
at the future
where my sight
and comprehension
would often be askew,
the magic of the body
preparing to saw
the Lady of Clarity.

I grabbed a paper
and remembered the Chinese
saying: Almost right
is good enough—
it cheered me.

When my wife
came out of the bank,
wearing her scarf
bright as red birds,
I asked if her credit card
problem had been solved
only to have her
remind me that it was
her debit card.

I almost thanked her
for the minor correction.

HEARING AID FOR THE YOUNGER

The nerves are dead, but the ear is bionic.
What you can pick up from afar
you lose close up. It's like a liaison
tucked inside an Amos Oz novel
where the couple tries to make love through a blanket.
The damn chirping birds drive you crazy—
You'd give your two arms to have
the human voice cause as much racket.
A woman says this makes you "distinguished,"
which you interpret to mean "You're going downhill
fast, faster, nothing left, exquisite or sexual."
No, you can't kid yourself: Eminent Miracle aside,
your ear will never again be efficient
as the blond ears of the Wehrmacht
as they rolled across France in a matter of days.
But then you're at home anyway among the refugees,
the battered angels, all those
who have to use sign language to tell you
"Oh listen, it's not so bad.
Turn up the volume and fuck it."

EVERY CITY THAT'S EVER BEEN

An organ grinder's monkey,
wearing its purple
jacket and hat.

Subways cackling under
the bone yards,
over the bridges.

A woman in a kimono,
stepping through the first
snow of the season.

Newspapers trashing the alley,
a book safely hidden
among the redroot.

The sun pasted between
high rises, miles of earth
and sky, a dress on a flagpole.

Every city that's ever been.

PASTA

After the news on a rather pleasant day
a saying from Bologna comes calling:
"Having spaghetti is better than having sex"
and while there's truth, much truth in this,
the reverse too has its fidelity. Still,
feasting with friends at a long table
is what one wag in the group
will label the lunchpin of existence.
The voracious talk, both high and low,
makes everyone potent, giddy.
The wine keeps flowing and why not?
Not one of us is guaranteed tomorrow.
As for the won't leave us alone question:
Who is it who will remember us?—
don't even attempt an answer. Forget it.
Take a walk in a place like Rome,
head in the direction of the carnival
you wanted to run away to
when you were a boy. Notice the woman
who is leaning far out her window.
"Federico," she says, "is flying over the city.
My god, how does the man do it?"
The entire skyline turns bright orange,
and through the tangle of leafless branches
look and see a horde of red balloons
rising to Heaven. Keep in mind
the promise of a hot plate of spaghetti
waiting for you in your new upstairs kitchen,
waiting for all the orphans
who have finally heard "Come and get it"—
this earthly dish so in love with our desire,
the big fork and the hungry heart,
as wholly, wholly delicious as a terrific life.

ABSOLUTELY

> *I don't want my legacy of happiness to die*
> —Pablo Neruda

There's not much chance,
despite all the times
my happiness has turned me
into Y. A. Tittle, bloody and bowed
on cold Soldier Field.

Only my love is perfect,
despite all the times
she's told me she's not—
proving that even she
doesn't know everything.

In my new old sneakers
I walk and walk.
If I had a clue where the hell
it was, I'd walk as close to heaven
as providence and my feet let me.

Here's to the rain mercifully
drowning out the gangsters
at City Hall—fall with me
on the couch, darling. Happiness
and its legacy need their rest too.

A MAN AND THE SERIOUS WORLD

His pants escape
and fall to his ankles.
He pulls them up,
this time holding on
from a ledge—until
he can cinch the belt
tight, just right.
Outside the world
is waiting, a world
with such a wealth
of embarrassments,
his contribution can be
drastically misunder-
stood. "I better be
on my toes," he says.

THE SOUND OF MONEY LEAVING

Lost quicker than a man can say chartreuse
and the time it takes to find his socks and shoes—
or his Stetson hat and silk-lined gloves
he undoubtedly had before the money disappeared
into the streets of wind and land
of forbidden prayers. Sour and sorrow show up
everywhere—dogs and cats turn into yaks
and ospreys—the sound of money leaving has this
strangeness, this imagination—ask any man
who waves it goodbye, who surrenders to the world
coming at him now like a hammerhead shark.

COUNTING ON ONE

The man and the boy in him
who both believed they'd reach the top
are experiencing the great leveler—
maybe even the descent has begun,
the lurking shadow of Icarus come
to gum up the works. All the things
they wished to accomplish has been
narrowed to one: "If I can do this
one thing, this one thing"—one decent
line for instance, and for the rest of their
life they'll pursue that perfection, hoping
this is the attainable one by flying lower
over the earth now, sometimes skimming
over the tops of the stinkweeds, the beautiful
but far too cautious lilies of the field.

EVEN IN PARIS

Those who not only
sought justice in their lifetime
but tried to live by its example
are living in Paris,

unlike those poor souls
who have to spend eternity
in cities like Bucharest.
Unseen, the virtuous ones

will occasionally help us
pour the wine, nudge us
to be overcome by beauty,
even provide counsel when a man's

Yvette says she's leaving, plane
ticket to LA in her pocket:
"Don't be absurd. Talk to her. No
sense living alone, even in Paris."

SPLENDID FOR THE NEW LIFE

A woman hovers in the sky—
it must be Spring.

A boy dreams of being President
or a grease monkey.

A man wants to write
about the woman hovering

in the sky and the boy
who keeps dreaming,

although the man has no desire
to be President. Better

the grease monkey, actually—
splendid for the new life

he feels slogging his way
every, everyday now.

DANCERS GOING FAR

They start dancing in the park
and continue down the avenues—
slipping in and out of traffic
like a couple of ruby eels.

They dance to the city's outskirts,
onto the Interstate—the truckers
at Joe's Diner cheering them on.
They travel a country road

to the ocean and dance
on the waves—toward a cruise ship
surrounded by an army of gulls,
toward France, content to be taking

the long way to Pluto—where
distant relatives are knitting
a cluster of stars, happy to have
the dancing fools back.

ON THE STREET LEADING TO THE MEAN STREETS

I watch the woman
in the jacket yellow as butter
until she passes
under a billboard:
EAST RIVER IS THE BANK FOR LOVERS
and I remind myself
how I know everything about love
and how I know nothing about it.
This is as it should be:
poetry is both rich and poor
all at the same time
and when I check my wallet
I see I'll have
enough bills to last the day
and I'll bet my last dollar
that tonight my dreams
will be bathed in yellow light,
my shoes awash in tiny stars
and wingtips of vast good fortune—
now even the most
dangerous streets are home.

AFTER THE ELECTION

I walk along the Delaware,
with no purpose nor ideology in mind,
far as I can tell.
The lights along the river
radiate like red evening gloves
worn by a beautiful woman.
A mile away is the diner
whose neon sign has been missing
a couple of letters long before
the candidates made a pit stop,
praising the cherry pie.

HONG KONG HUI

The Hui brothers—
Michael, Samuel, Ricky—
are plying their nonsense
on the screen.
They're so zany
you have to laugh,
no matter what
you've been through.
Like The Three Stooges.
Like our lives.
Exactly like our lives.

THE PRESENT AND THE FUTURE

A grand design is emerging.
There are no marching bands
no women waving flags
no men cheering
with beer glasses in their hands,
but everything is changing,
everything I wanted to be
awash in the branches of trees,
chips sprinkling down like confetti,
covering the streets
with a beautiful ash.
Catch me sitting on a cheap
lawn chair in front
of a brownstone—a poor man's
Buddha watching the world
go by with the noise
from the nearby canal
diminishing like cherry blossoms.
Take all the time necessary,
over a million years
if you'd like. I'll be here.
I'll be here, waiting for you.

About the Author

Tim Suermondt has published two chapbooks and a full-length collection of poems, *Trying To Help The Elephant Man Dance* from Backwaters Press, 2007. He's had poems in many magazines and online, including: *The New York Quarterly, Poetry, The Georgia Review, Poetry Northwest, Poetry East, Blackbird, Barrow Street, Bellevue Literary Review* and *Stand Magazine* (U.K.)—and poems in *Poetry After 9/11: An Anthology of New York Poets* (Melville House Publications, 2002) and *Visiting Walt* (a Whitman anthology from the University of Iowa Press, 2003.) He lives in Brooklyn with his wife, the poet Pui Ying Wong.

About NYQ Books™

NYQ Books™ was established in 2009 as an imprint of The New York Quarterly Foundation, Inc. Its mission is to augment the New York Quarterly poetry magazine by providing an additional venue for poets already published in the magazine. A lifelong dream of NYQ's founding editor, William Packard, NYQ Books™ has been made possible by both growing foundation support and new technology that was not available during William Packard's lifetime. We are proud to present these books to you and hope that you will continue to support The New York Quarterly Foundation, Inc. and our poets and that you will enjoy these other titles from NYQ Books™:

Joanna Crispi	Soldier in the Grass
Pui Ying Wong	Yellow Plum Season
Ted Jonathan	Bones and Jokes
Fred Yannantuono	A Boilermaker for the Lady
Amanda J. Bradley	Hints and Allegations
Grace Zabriskie	Poems

Please visit our website for these and other titles:

www.nyqbooks.org

www.ingramcontent.com/pod-product-compliance
Lightning Source LLC
LaVergne TN
LVHW011426080426
835512LV00005B/294